I Hate the Word "BULLY"

A Story That Teach Kids How to Stop Being Bullied

David Fletcher

Copyright

Copyright © 2022 David Fletcher.

All rights reserved. This book or any portion thereof may not be reproduced or used in any manner whatsoever without the express written permission of the publisher except for the use of brief quotations in a book review.

THIS
book belongs to

NAME:

AGE:

SAYING HURTFUL THINGS

MAKING YOU DO THINGS YOU DON'T WANT TO

TRYING TO HURT YOU PHYSICALLY

STOPPING YOU FROM JOINING IN WITH GAMES AND ACTIVITIES WITH OTHERS

GIVING NASTY LOOKS OR MAKING RUDE SIGNS

IF SOMEONE DOES THIS ONLY ONCE OR TWICE IT IS NOT CALLED BULLYING BUT IT IS STILL NOT OK.

TELL A TEACHER

TELL A PARENT

NO ONE SHOULD BE BULLIED.

IF YOU THINK YOU ARE BEING BULLIED YOU SHOULD TELL AN ADULT.

TELLING AN ADULT MEANS THAT THEY CAN TRY TO HELP YOU STOP THE BULLYING.

NOTES

NOTES

NOTES

Printed in Great Britain
by Amazon